❖ GREAT LITTLE COOK

Spanish COOKING

Marianne Kaltenbach

Spanish holiday eating at home

Who does not enjoy reminiscing about evenings with delicate tapas, a traditional paella and a carafe of red wine? Dream no longer! With these original recipes from all regions of Spain you can fulfil your wish in the most delightful way. And you will find your guests are enthusiastic too. Buen provecho – enjoy yourself!

The colour photographs are by Odette Teubner and Kerstin Mosny.

AURA

CONTENTS

Eating and drinking in Spain 4

Spanish cooking 4
Culinary regions 4
Historical influences 5
Spanish eating customs 6
A typical cena 6
Drinks with meals 6
Festivals and special occasions 6
Bringing Spain to your kitchen 7
Buen provecho! 7

Tapas, starters and salads 8

Marinated anchovies 8
Boquerones al vinagre 8
Tomato bread with anchovy fillets 8
Pan y tomate con anchoas
Tuna with tomatoes and peppers 10
Pimiento, tomate y atún
Lemon potatoes 10
Patatas al limón
Spicy meatballs 10
Albondigas
Chicken croquettes 12
Croquetas de pollo
Cooked vegetable salad 12
Escalivada
Mixed salad 14
Ensalada mista

Soups and stews 16

Monkfish soup 16
Sopa de rape
Onion soup 16
Sopa de cebolla
Minorcan fish soup 18
Caldera menorquina
Chick pea hotpot 18
Cocido de garbanzos
Lamb stew with haricot beans 20
Cordero con judías blancas
Fisherman's stew 22
Suquet de pescado
Barcelona fish hotpot 22
Zarzuela

Eggs, pasta and rice dishes 24

Basque-style omelette 24
Piperrada a la vasca
Spanish-style potato tortilla 24
Tortilla de patatas a la española
Macaroni Basque-style 26
Macarrones a la vasca
Baked pasta rolls 26
Canalones
Paella 26
Rice Cuban-style 28
Arroz a la cubana
Black rice 30
Arroz negro

Fish and seafood 32

Sea bream Madrid-style 32
Besugo a la madrileña
Gilt-headed bream in a salt crust 32
Dorada al la sal
Hake with green sauce 32
Merluza a la vasca
Trout Pyrenean-style 34
Truchas al estilo del Pirineo
Monkfish fisherman-style 35
Rape a la marinera
Baked fish 36
Pescado al horno

Meat and poultry dishes 42

Fried squid 38
Calamares a la romana
Small grilled squid 38
Pulpitos a la plancha
Mussels Catalan-style 40
Mejillones a la catalana
Shellfish with yellow sauce 40
Almejas con salsa amarilla
Leg of lamb Castillian-style 42
Pierna de cordero asado a la castellana
Veal with peppers 42
Estufado de ternera con pimientos
Rice with rabbit 43
Arroz con conejo 44
Roast chicken with vegetables 46
Pollo en xanfaina
Chicken with almond sauce 46
Gallina en pepitoria
Chicken with crayfish 46
Pollo con langosta 48
Pigs' trotters with pine nuts 50
Pies de cerdo con piñones
Tripe Madrid-style 50
Callos a la madrileña

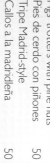

Vegetable dishes 52
Aubergines with cheese
Berenjenas con queso 52
Aubergine moulds
Pastel de berenjenas 52
Spinach with raisins and pine nuts 54
Espinacas con pasas y piñones
Beans and peas Mallorca-style
Verdura con huevos a la 54
mallorquina

Stuffed peppers
Pimientos rellenos 58
guipuzcoanos
Aubergines with honey 56
Berenjenas con miel 56

Puddings and tarts 58

Fried bananas 58
Platanos fritos

Catalan cream
Crema catalana 58
Apricot cream
Crema de albaricoques 58
Fig tart with almonds 60
Tarta de higos con almendras
Apple tart with brandy 60
Tarta de manzana al coñac

Index 62

EATING AND DRINKING IN SPAIN

Spanish cooking

As with the cuisines of most countries, there is no such thing as 'Spanish cooking'. Every region of Spain has its own culinary specialities and particular ways of preparing food, depending on its topography, weather and local produce, and these have remained almost unchanged for generations. When you travel through the different regions, you will realize with surprise the great variety and versatility of Spanish cooking.

Nevertheless, there are what might be termed national dishes, often prepared for celebrations and special occasions. Game is popular throughout Spain and many dishes are flavoured with sherry. Beef is a feature of the North, while Southerners tend to eat more pork. Sweet pastries, featuring large quantities of sugar and almonds, are eaten virtually everywhere.

With the advent of tourism, the quality and type of food available has changed, but Spain has always adapted traditions from other parts of the world. The Moorish conquest introduced rice to Spain. Cooking with chocolate is a legacy of the days when Mexico was a Spanish colony. The other countries of Europe owe a debt of gratitude to Spain for introducing chillies and tomatoes to their cuisines.

Culinary regions

Interest in Spanish regional cuisine has grown massively in recent years and there are now many restaurants that have earned worldwide reputations for their local Spanish specialities. You could fill a whole book by describing all the regional variations and specialities, so here I have confined myself to the most important and best-known regions of the country with their typical dishes.

Cataluña

Here you will find substantial country cooking, which generally uses quite a lot of olive oil. The region also includes the rather more elegant and sophisticated cooking of the great cities of Barcelona and Tarragona.

Three basic preparation methods are typical of the region: the *sofrito*, a very concentrated tomato-and-onion purée, the *xanfaina*, braised peppers, courgettes, aubergines, onions and tomatoes, and the *picada*, a mixture of almonds, garlic and fresh parsley.

The Balearic Islands

The cookery of these islands – Mallorca, Minorca, Ibiza and others – is influenced by the cookery of Valencia and Cataluña. Hardly surprisingly, fish dishes of every conceivable variety are particular favourites. Just two examples are *Caldora menorquina*, Minorcan fish soup and *torta de sardinas*, a kind of sardine pizza.

Andalusia

The most famous dish of this region is *gazpacho*, a chilled tomato soup, pleasantly refreshing in the heat of summer. In fact, it has become the model for chilled soups throughout the world. Andalusian cooking is versatile and attractive, both on the coast and especially in the historic cities of Granada, Córdoba and Seville.

Many Spanish housewives take it for granted they can buy freshly caught fish and seafood straight from the fisherman. The kinds of fish available vary according to region and season, but some kind of seafood, from prawns to squid and from sardines to sea bream, is on a typical Spanish menu at any time.

traditions are firmly entrenched, particularly in country districts. Families have cooked in the same way for centuries, so it is worth taking a quick look at the history of Iberian cookery.

The influences of foreign cultures can be traced back to the Roman Empire under Julius Caesar. The Romans brought two important foods to Spain: olive oil and garlic. Even then, the healthy properties of these two ingredients were appreciated and they soon became indispensable to Spanish cooking. The Romans loved substantial, strongly spiced dishes that had been braised for a long time. This tradition is still evident today. The Arab invasion brought new spices to Spain – saffron, cinnamon and nutmeg. The Arabs also brought previously unknown vegetables: the artichoke and *nabos*, small white turnips, which were crossed with varieties of cabbage to produce large turnips. Contact with the countries it had conquered also influenced Spanish cuisine. Chocolate came to Spain from the New World and it was used not only for drinks and sweet desserts, but also for savoury sauces. Neighbouring countries also had their effect on Spanish cooking traditions. The cookery of southern France has clearly left its mark in Cataluña. The influence of the French Basque country can be felt in northern Spain, particularly in fish recipes. Portuguese influence is

Garlic lovers will really enjoy Spanish cooking because it is used often and abundantly.

Valencia
The Arabs brought rice to this region and it is still the hallmark of its cuisine. Its most famous rice dish is, of course, *paella valenciana*, which can be sampled in innumerable variations throughout the region. It may contain almost any combination of chicken, pork, duck, fish, seafood and spicy sausages, as well as vegetables and pulses.

Madrid
For most Spaniards, the cuisine of the capital is the best in the country. Hearty hotpots with meat, vegetables and offal are characteristic and other typical dishes include *Tortilla de patatas a la española*, Spanish-style potato tortilla, and *Callos a la madrileña*, Tripe Madrid-style.

The Basque country
For me the cuisine of this region is the best because it is particularly easy and versatile. Specialities to be recommended are fish and seafood dishes, such as *Bacalao a la viscaina*, cod with dried peppers, and *Merluza en salsa verde*, hake with green sauce.

Historical influences
However, despite all these regional variations, there are common national features in Spanish cooking. Many cooking

perceptible on the frontier and the cuisine of the Canary Islands is sometimes inspired by South American cooking traditions.

Spanish eating customs

As in all southern countries, breakfast in Spain tends to be modest. Spaniards usually drink coffee or hot chocolate for breakfast and like to eat some kind of cake or sweet pastry with it. Those doing physical work may have a rather more substantial second 'breakfast' at about eleven o'clock. Then they eat fried

Spanish jerez or sherry is stored in these wooden barrels until it acquires its incomparable flavour.

sausage, tortilla or pâté. The *comida*, lunch, is eaten very late, usually between two and three o'clock in the afternoon. It often consists of a salad with vegetables, meat or sausage, a soup or a hotpot. Early evening is the time for *tapas*, small cocktail snacks made with olives, sausages or seafood. These are available in every bar. Sweet snacks are often sold from street stalls, the most famous being *churros*, a sort of doughnut. The main meal of the day, over which Spaniards like to spend several hours, is the *cena*, supper, for which people traditionally gather at about ten o'clock at night.

A typical cena

To start with there are small appetizers: tapas, salad, sausage or bacon. Then comes a nourishing starter, such as a tortilla or a paella. The next course – depending on the region – is a fish or meat dish, roast poultry or rabbit. Between courses smaller dishes, such as snails, may be served. At the end there is cheese, fruit, dessert or cake. Particular favourites are *Crema catalana* and *flan*, an egg custard with caramel sauce. Finally, there is strong black coffee, possibly with brandy.

Drinks with meals

The choice of drinks to accompany meals is very important in Spain. People may drink a glass of sherry with tapas – preferably in a bar, chatting with friends and acquaintances. A dry white wine is served with starters, followed by a rosé or red, depending on the type of main dish. The most famous and best Spanish wines come from the Rioja region and from Navarre. Previously the sweet wine of Malaga was a favourite, but today it is mostly used to accompany desserts. Spaniards also like to drink beer, especially with substantial hotpots and meat dishes.

Festivals and special occasions

Eating together with the whole family on Sundays and feast days has a special significance.

original recipes without difficulty, I have taken care to use only ingredients that are widely available or can be found in good specialist food shops or delicatessens. Alternatives are suggested for more unusual ingredients that are difficult to find outside Spain. In addition, I have 'slimmed down' many of the recipes and reduced the quantity of oil used to suit our taste. Do not further reduce the quantity of oil specified in the recipe or the dish will lose its typical flavour. I have also cut down many of the cooking times – particularly of vegetables – which benefits many dishes. However, shorter cooking times cannot be recommended for all the meals. Specialities, such as braised dishes, soups and hotpots, must be cooked for a long time to allow the flavours of their individual ingredients to mingle.

It is worth buying the best-quality olive oil. Extra virgin oil is produced by the first cold pressing and has the best flavour. It is expensive, but the difference is noticeable. Virgin olive oil, also cold pressed, is a little less expensive and has a fine flavour, but a slightly higher acidity than extra virgin. Other types, usually simply labelled 'pure', are refined and may have been heat-treated.

Buen provecho!

So much for Spanish cooking. It only remains for me to wish you a good appetite or *Buen provecho!* as they say in Spain.

Olives and olive oil play a very important part in Spanish cooking – as in all Mediterranean cookery. To ensure authenticity, it is particularly important to be sure to use really good quality oil.

Each region serves typical traditional dishes on particular festivals, such as Easter, Christmas and New Year. The almost universal dish prepared on Good Friday is *bacalao*, salt cod with peppers and tomatoes. Christmas is especially festive. Christmas Eve is virtually a fast-day; only a light meal, usually consisting of fish, is served. On Christmas Day, however, the table is laden with festive food. A typical Christmas meal in Cataluña, for example, offers *escudella*, a very rich pot roast consisting of various kinds of meat, black pudding and vegetables. Traditionally, the next course is usually poultry – chicken, duck or capon – stuffed with small fried sausages and pine nuts. The final sweet course consists of *turón*, a sumptuous dessert with nougat.

Bringing Spain to your kitchen

For the last 25 years I have spent one to two months in Spain each year and have often been invited to eat in people's homes. Consequently, over the course of time, I have come to know the different cuisines of each region and collected countless original recipes. To ensure that you can follow the

Marinated anchovies

Boquerones al vinagre

Easy

Serves 4
400 g/14 oz cleaned fresh anchovies
200 ml/7 fl oz white wine vinegar
2 cloves garlic
1 bunch parsley
30 ml/2 tablespoons olive oil
salt and freshly ground black pepper

Approximately per portion:
860 kJ/200 kcal
21 g protein, 15 g fat
2 g carbohydrate

● Approximate preparation time: 12½ hours of which 12 hours are marinating time

---

I. Slit the anchovies lengthways from head to tail using a sharp knife. Carefully pull the tail fins towards the head to remove the backbone. Wash the anchovy fillets under cold running water and pat thoroughly dry with absorbent kitchen paper.

2. Put the anchovy fillets into a shallow, non-metallic bowl and pour the white wine vinegar over them. Cover with clear film and set aside in the refrigerator to marinate for about 12 hours.

3. Before serving drain the anchovies well and pat them dry with absorbent kitchen paper, then arrange them in portions in small bowls. Season to taste with a little salt and pepper.

4. Finely chop the garlic and chop the parsley. Mix together the garlic and parsley and sprinkle the mixture over the anchovies. Drizzle the olive oil over the fish and serve with cocktail sticks to eat them with.

Tip

The anchovies are even tastier if you add a small hot red pepper or a selection of mixed fresh herbs. Fresh anchovies are difficult to obtain outside the Mediterranean. You could substitute fresh sardines or even small herrings instead.

Tomato bread with anchovy fillets

Pan y tomate con anchoas

Quick

Serves 4
4 small tomatoes
4 cloves garlic
4–8 slices French bread, according to size
45–60 ml/3–4 tablespoons olive oil
12 canned anchovy fillets in oil
12 green olives, stuffed with pimientos
salt and freshly ground black pepper

Approximately per portion:
1,500 kJ/360 kcal
11 g protein, 25 g fat
26 g carbohydrate

● Approximate preparation time: 15 minutes

I. Briefly blanch the tomatoes, drain, then peel and cut them in half. Remove the seeds, put the tomato halves in a bowl and mash the flesh with a fork.

2. Crush the garlic and add to the tomatoes.

3. Toast the bread slices on both sides until light golden brown.

4. Spread the tomato and garlic mixture on the toast. Season to taste with a little salt and pepper and drizzle with the olive oil.

5. Drain the anchovy fillets well. Arrange an anchovy fillet in a small ring on top of each piece of toast, with an olive in the middle.

Variation
You can put a thin slice of jamón Serrano, sweet Spanish ham, or chorizo, spicy Spanish sausage, on top of the tomato toast. Instead of white bread, you can use rustic brown bread.

Above: Marinated anchovies
Below: Tomato bread with anchovy fillets

Tuna with tomatoes and peppers

Pimiento, tomate y atún

Exquisite

Serves 4

1 green pepper
4 ripe tomatoes
90 ml/6 tablespoons olive oil
30 ml/2 tablespoons pine nuts
5 ml/1 teaspoon sugar
200 g/7 oz can tuna in oil
salt

Approximately per portion:
2,100 kJ/500 kcal
13 g protein, 45 g fat
7 g carbohydrate

● Approximate preparation time: 45 minutes

1. Core and seed the green pepper and dice the flesh into 2.5 cm/1 inch cubes.

2. Briefly blanch the tomatoes in boiling water. Drain, then peel and dice the flesh.

3. Heat 15 ml/1 tablespoon of the olive oil in a heavy-based frying pan. Add the pine nuts and fry over a low heat, stirring constantly, until golden. Remove the pine nuts from the pan with a slotted spoon and set aside.

4. Add the remaining olive oil to the frying pan. Add the green pepper and sauté briefly. Then add the tomatoes.

5. Cook the vegetables over a low heat, stirring occasionally, for about 15 minutes, until the cooking juices have completely evaporated. Stir in the sugar and season to taste with a little salt.

6. Drain the tuna well and add it to the vegetables. Simmer the mixture for about 3 minutes, until heated through. Transfer to warm individual serving plates, sprinkle with the toasted pine nuts and serve immediately.

Lemon potatoes

Patatas al limón

Rather time-consuming

Serves 4

800 g/1³/4 lb small potatoes
2 lemons
15 ml/1 tablespoon white
    wine vinegar
30 ml/2 tablespoons beef stock
15 ml/1 tablespoon brandy
1 bunch parsley
8 cloves garlic
90 ml/6 tablespoons olive oil
salt and freshly ground
    black pepper

Approximately per portion:
2,000 kJ/480 kcal
6 g protein, 30 g fat
41 g carbohydrate

● Approximate preparation time: 50 minutes

1. Cook the potatoes in their skins in a small quantity of boiling salted water in a covered saucepan for about 25 minutes.

2. Drain, set aside to cool slightly, then peel them. While they are still lukewarm, cut them into ³/4 inch slices and arrange in a serving dish.

3. Squeeze the lemons. Put the juice into a bowl and stir in the wine vinegar, beef stock and brandy. Finely chop the parsley and add it to the bowl. Season the mixture to taste with salt and pepper and mix thoroughly.

4. Finely chop the garlic and add it to the lemon sauce, together with the olive oil. Beat together thoroughly with a whisk.

5. Pour the sauce over the lukewarm potatoes and serve immediately as a starter.

Tip

Instead of garlic, you can use chopped onions or shallots.

Above: Tuna with tomatoes and peppers
Below: Lemon potatoes

Spicy meatballs

Albondigas

Easy

Serves 8

2 large onions
60 ml/4 tablespoons olive oil
300 g/11 oz minced beef
300 g/11 oz minced veal or pork
30 ml/2 tablespoons breadcrumbs
3 large eggs
salt and freshly ground
black pepper
flour, for dusting

Approximately per portion:
1,700 kJ/405 kcal
20 g protein, 31 g fat
11 g carbohydrate

• Approximate preparation
time: 50 minutes

1. Finely chop the onions. Heat
30 ml/2 tablespoons of the olive
oil in a large frying pan. Add the
onions and sauté for 3–5 minutes,
until soft and translucent. Remove
the pan from the heat and transfer
the onion to a mixing bowl.

2. Add the minced beef, minced
pork or veal, breadcrumbs and
1 egg to the onions. Season to
taste with salt and pepper and mix
thoroughly. Form the mixture into
a ball, cover with clear film and set
aside in the refrigerator for about
30 minutes.

3. Divide the mixture into small,
equal-size portions on a lightly
floured work surface and with
floured hands, shape each portion
into small balls about 2.5 cm/1 inch
in diameter.

4. Sprinkle the meatballs with
sifted flour. Lightly beat the
remaining eggs and coat each
meatball with beaten egg. Heat the
remaining olive oil and fry the
meatballs, a few at a time, turning
frequently, for about 5 minutes,
until they are golden brown. Drain
thoroughly and keep warm while
you cook the remaining meatballs.
Transfer to warm serving plates
and serve immediately.

Chicken croquettes

Croquetas de pollo

Exquisite

Serves 4

1 large onion
50 g/2 oz lard
50 g/2 oz boiled bacon
250 g/9 oz boneless cooked chicken
60 ml/4 tablespoons flour
300 ml/1/2 pint milk
freshly grated nutmeg
50 g/2 oz butter
90 g/3½ oz crushed crispbread
or breadcrumbs
2 eggs
60 ml/4 tablespoons groundnut oil
salt and freshly ground black pepper

Approximately per portion:
3,300 kJ/790 kcal
27 g protein, 58 g fat
38 g carbohydrate

• Approximate preparation
time: 2³/4 hours of which
2 hours are cooling time

1. Finely chop the onion. Melt
the lard in a large, heavy-based
frying pan. Add the onion and
sauté for 3–5 minutes, until it is
soft and translucent.

2. Dice or mince the bacon and
chicken and mix together. Add the
chicken mixture to the pan and fry,
stirring constantly, for about
3 minutes.

3. Stir in the flour, then add the
milk. Keep stirring until the mixture
becomes firm. If necessary, add
more milk.

4. Remove the frying pan from the
heat and season the mixture to
taste with nutmeg, salt and pepper.
Dice the butter and stir it in. Set
aside to cool. Then chill in the
refrigerator for about 2 hours.

5. Put the crushed crispbread or
breadcrumbs on a plate. Lightly
beat the eggs and pour them on to
a flat plate.

6. Form small balls or sausage-
shaped croquettes from the
cooled chicken mixture between
the palms of your hands. Dip the
croquettes first in the beaten
eggs, then in the crispbread
crumbs or breadcrumbs.

7. Heat the oil in a frying pan.
Add the croquettes and fry,
turning frequently, for about
5 minutes, until they are golden
brown all over. Transfer to a warm
serving dish and serve immediately.

*Above: Chicken croquettes
Below: Spicy meatballs*

Cooked vegetable salad

Escalivada

This salad's name comes from the verb *escalivar*, meaning to cook on hot ashes. This cooking method gives the escalivada its particular char-grilled flavour, but if you do not have a barbecue, it can also be cooked very successfully in a conventional oven.

Rather time-consuming

Serves 4

2 large aubergines
4 red peppers
90 ml/6 tablespoons extra virgin olive oil
2 cloves garlic
salt

Approximately per portion:
1,400 kJ/330 kcal
3 g protein, 30 g fat
9 g carbohydrate
• Approximate preparation time: 1 1/4 hours

1. Cook the aubergines and peppers over glowing hot charcoal on a barbecue or in a preheated oven at 180°C/350°F/ Gas 4 until the skins are charred and beginning to blister.

2. Put the aubergines and peppers into a bowl, cover and set aside for about 15 minutes.

3. Peel, core and seed the red peppers and cut the flesh into strips about 2.5 cm/1 inch wide.

Peel the aubergines and cut them lengthways into slices about 2 cm/3/4 inch thick.

4. Put the pepper strips and aubergine slices into a shallow bowl, sprinkle with a little salt and pour the olive oil over them. Finely chop the garlic and sprinkle it over the vegetables. Serve warm.

Variation

You can also mix the vegetables with potatoes and onions. Sauté thin slices of potato and strips of onion in olive oil and then mix them with the prepared peppers and aubergines. You could also use mixed red and yellow peppers.

Mixed salad

Ensalada mista

In Spain salad is always served without a dressing. People mix their own dressing from olive oil and wine vinegar at the table. Always use good-quality extra virgin olive oil for salads.

Easy

Serves 4

4 spring onions
1 stick celery
3 tomatoes
1 red pepper
1 lettuce
2 hard-boiled eggs
8 black olives
wine vinegar
extra virgin olive oil
salt and freshly ground black pepper
2–3 bottled or canned artichoke hearts, to garnish

Approximately per portion:
850 kJ/200 kcal
8 g protein, 13 g fat
13 g carbohydrate
• Approximate preparation time: 15 minutes

1. Thinly slice the spring onions into rings. Thinly slice the celery. Cut the tomatoes into slices about 1 cm/1/2 inch thick.

2. Core and seed the peppers and cut the flesh into strips. Wash the lettuce and shake dry. Shell the eggs and cut them in half.

3. Arrange the tomato slices, lettuce leaves, peppers, spring onions, celery, olives and halved eggs on individual serving plates. Drain the artichoke hearts, cut them in half and use them to garnish the salad.

4. Serve the salad at room temperature, together with the wine vinegar, olive oil, salt and black pepper.

Above: Cooked vegetable salad
Below: Mixed salad

SOUPS AND STEWS

Monkfish soup

Sopa de rape

The recipe for this soup comes from Cataluña.

Exquisite

Serves 4

For the fish stock:
500 g/1¼ lb fish bones and heads
1 sprig celery leaves
1 bay leaf
2.5 ml/½ teaspoon dried thyme
2.5 ml/½ teaspoon dried oregano
500 g/1¼ lb prepared monkfish tail
30 ml/2 tablespoons black
   peppercorns

For the soup:
1 litre/1¾ pints water
200 g/7 oz white bread
1 large onion
3 large ripe tomatoes
2 cloves garlic
90 ml/6 tablespoons olive oil
10 shelled almonds
pinch of saffron
pinch of ground cinnamon
salt and freshly ground black pepper

Approximately per portion:
3,200 kJ/760 kcal
41 g protein, 40 g fat
57 g carbohydrate
● Approximate preparation time: 1 hour

1. Put the fish bones and heads into a large saucepan with the celery leaves, bay leaf, thyme, oregano and 200 g/7 oz of the monkfish. Crush the peppercorns and add them. Add the water and bring to the boil.

2. Dice 115 g/4 oz of the white bread, put it into a bowl, ladle a little of the fish stock over it and set aside. Chop the onion. Briefly blanch the tomatoes in boiling water. Peel the tomatoes and dice the flesh. Crush 1 garlic clove. Heat 30 ml/2 tablespoons of the olive oil. Add the onion, crushed garlic and tomatoes and sauté over a medium heat for about 10 minutes.

3. Dry-fry the almonds in a heavy-based frying pan, turning frequently, over a medium heat. Remove them from the pan and crush them in a mortar or finely chop them in a food processor.

4. Finely chop the remaining garlic and add it to the almonds, together with the saffron. Pound the mixture all to a fine paste and stir in 15–30 ml/1–2 tablespoons of the fish stock.

Variation

In Andalusia, rice is added to this soup and it is seasoned with paprika.

Tip

In Spain the large fleshy head of the monkfish is usually cooked in the stock and is then passed through a fine strainer. As we can seldom obtain monkfish head here, I have substituted some of the tail. You can also use a more economical fish, such as cod, for the stock.

5. Pour the fish stock through a fine strainer and return to the saucepan. Discard the flavourings, fish bones and heads, but reserve the monkfish.

6. Put the cooked monkfish in a food processor, together with the softened bread and a little of the stock and process until smooth. Mix together the monkfish paste and fried tomatoes. Add this mixture to the reserved fish stock and bring to the boil again. Add the almond paste and simmer for about 10 minutes.

7. Finely dice the remaining monkfish and marinate it in 15 ml/1 tablespoon of the remaining olive oil for about 5 minutes. Meanwhile, finely dice the remaining white bread. Heat the remaining olive oil, add the diced bread and fry over a medium heat until golden brown. Season the soup to taste with cinnamon, salt and pepper.

8. Add the diced monkfish to the soup and heat through for about 5 minutes. Ladle the soup into individual warm bowls and serve with the fried croûtons.

Onion soup

Sopa de cebolla

Easy

Serves 4

1.2 kg/2 lb 10 oz onions
50 g/2 oz lard
1.2 litres/2 pints beef stock
30 ml/2 tablespoons brandy
salt and freshly ground black pepper

- Approximate preparation
  time: 1 hour

Approximately per portion:
1,000 kJ/240 kcal
5 g protein, 15 g fat
20 g carbohydrate

1. Cut the onions into thin strips.
Heat the lard in a large saucepan.
Add the onions and fry over a
medium heat for about 3 minutes,
until they begin to colour.

2. Add the stock and bring to the
boil. Cover and simmer over a low
heat for about 20 minutes.

3. Rub the onion soup through a
fine strainer or process it in a food
processor to make a purée. Stir in
the brandy and season to taste
with a little salt and pepper. Bring
to the boil again and simmer for a
further 20 minutes. Ladle the soup
into a warm tureen or individual
soup bowls and serve immediately.

Minorcan fish soup

Caldera menorquina

Can be prepared in advance

Serves 4

1 large onion
3 tomatoes
3 cloves garlic
1 kg/2 1/4 lb fish fillets, such as
monkfish or bream
750 ml/1 1/4 pints water
45 ml/3 tablespoons olive oil
8 thin slices white bread
5 ml/1 teaspoon mild paprika
1/2 bunch parsley
salt

- Approximate preparation
  time: 40 minutes

1. Finely chop the onions. Cut the
tomatoes into quarters. Cut the
the garlic. Put the onions,
tomatoes and garlic into large,
heavy-based saucepan.

2. Cut the fish into 2.5 cm/1 inch
chunks and add to the saucepan.

3. Pour in the water and olive oil.
The fish should be covered with
liquid, so if necessary, add more
water. Bring the soup to the boil,
then reduce the heat. Cover and
simmer for about 20 minutes, until
the fish is cooked.

4. Meanwhile, toast the bread and
put 2 slices into the base of each
of 4 individual soup bowls.
Remove the cooked fish chunks
from the soup, set aside and keep
them warm. Bring the soup back
to the boil and season to taste
with salt and pepper. Chop the
parsley and add it to the soup.
Pour the soup on the toasted
bread in the soup bowls and serve
immediately. Serve the cooked fish
separately. Alternatively, just before
serving, heat it again in the soup
and serve both together.

Tip

If you use a mixture of different
kinds of fish for the soup,
remember that they may have
different cooking times. Add
them separately to the soup
and cook each for the
appropriate length of time.

*Above: Onion soup
Below: Minorcan fish soup*

Chick pea hotpot

Cocido de garbanzos

Rather time-consuming

Serves 4

400 g/14 oz chick peas
500 ml/17 fl oz water
1 ham bone or 200 g/7 oz belly
of pork
1 pig's ear
1 pig's tail
3 large potatoes
salt

Approximately per portion:
2,800 kJ/670 kcal
36 g protein, 34 g fat
56 g carbohydrate

● Approximate preparation
time: 14 hours of which
12 hours are soaking time

1. The day before the soup is
required, put the chick peas into a
bowl, add a little salt and the
water. Set aside to soak for
12 hours.

2. Put the chick peas and their
soaking water into a large
saucepan and bring to the boil.
Add the ham bone, pig's ear and
tail. Cover and simmer over a
medium heat for 60–80 minutes. If
necessary, add more hot water.

3. Dice the potatoes and add to
pan. Cook for about 30 minutes,
until tender.

4. Remove the ham bone and
serve the hotpot immediately.

Tip

Pig's ear and tail were once
widely available, but now are
seen only rarely. It is worth
ordering them from your
butcher, as both are rich and
gelatinous. Both must be
thoroughly washed and the ears
should be singed before use.

Lamb stew with haricot beans

Cordero con judias blancas

Rather time-consuming

Serves 6

400 g/14 oz haricot beans
1 litre/1³/4 pints sparkling
mineral water
1 small celeriac
2 onions
3 cloves garlic
250 g/9 oz can tomatoes
150 g/5 oz smoked bacon
30 ml/2 tablespoons olive oil
600 g/1 lb 5 oz boneless shoulder
of lamb
1 leek
5 ml/1 teaspoon dried thyme
salt and freshly ground black pepper

● Approximate preparation
time: 14¹/2 hours of which
12 hours are soaking time

1. On the day before the stew is
required, put the haricot beans
into a bowl, together with the
mineral water and set aside to
soak for 12 hours.

2. Drain the beans and discard the
soaking water. Put the beans into a
large saucepan and add enough
cold water to cover them by about
2.5 cm/1 inch. Bring to the boil and
skim off the scum.

3. Peel the celeriac and cut it in
half. Add 1 onion, 1 celeriac half,
1 clove garlic and the tomatoes to
the saucepan.

4. Dice the bacon. Cut the lamb
into 2.5 cm/1 inch cubes. Heat the
olive oil in a large saucepan. Add
the bacon and lamb and fry,
stirring frequently, until the lamb is
browned all over.

5. Chop the remaining onion and
dice the remaining celeriac. Cut
the leek lengthways into quarters
and then across into 4 chunks. Add
the chopped onion, diced celeriac
and the leek to the lamb and sauté
for about 5 minutes. Crush the
remaining garlic and add to the
pan. Stir in the thyme and season
to taste with salt and pepper.

6. Strain the beans and add them
to the meat. Discard the
vegetables in the strainer. Pour in
enough water to cover the beans.
Cover the saucepan and cook for
about 1 hour, until the meat and
beans are tender.

Above: Chick pea hotpot
Below: Lamb stew with haricot beans

Fisherman's stew

Suquet de pescado

Exquisite

Serves 4
1 large onion
250 g/9 oz mussels
4 raw langoustines
4 raw Mediterranean prawns
120 ml/4 fl oz olive oil,
1 large tomato
3 cloves garlic
45–60 ml/3–4 tablespoons water
2 teaspoons paprika
2 cod steaks
4 monkfish steaks
salt and freshly ground black pepper

Approximately per portion:
2,400 kJ/560 kcal
23 g protein, 12 g fat
16 g carbohydrate

● Approximate preparation time: 35 minutes

1. Chop the onion. Debeard and scrub the mussels, discarding any that remain open. Peel and devein the langoustines and prawns.

2. Heat the oil in a large pan. Fry the onion, langoustines and prawns, stirring frequently, for 3 minutes. Remove the seafood.

3. Blanch, peel and chop the tomatoes. Chop the garlic. Pound the tomatoes and garlic together. Add the tomatoes to the onions and stir in the water. Add the fish and stir in the mussels, cover and cook, shaking the pan occasionally, for 5 minutes. Discard any mussels that have not opened. Add the langoustines and prawns and cook for 3 minutes, Stir in the paprika and season to taste with salt and pepper before serving.

Barcelona fish hotpot

Zarzuela

Exquisite • Rather expensive

Serves 4
500 g/1 1/4 lb fish bones
500 ml/17 fl oz water
2 large onions
1 fresh red chilli
4 large mussels
4 langoustines
4 tiger prawns
60 ml/4 tablespoons olive oil
2 small prepared squid
45 ml/3 tablespoons tomato purée
5 cloves garlic
4 slices monkfish
250 ml/8 fl oz white wine
10 shelled almonds
4 slices crispbread
15 ml/1 tablespoon aniseed liqueur
1 small sprig rosemary
1 bunch parsley
salt and freshly ground black pepper

Approximately per portion:
2,500 kJ/600 kcal
53 g protein, 25 g fat
28 g carbohydrate

● Approximate preparation time: 1 1/4 hours

1. Put the fish bones and water in a large saucepan, bring to the boil, cover and simmer for 10 minutes. Strain the stock and return to the pan. Bring back to the boil and simmer for a further 10 minutes.

2. Chop the onions and finely chop the chilli. Debeard and scrub the mussels. Discard any that remain open. Peel and devein the langoustines and prawns. Heat 30 ml/2 tablespoons of the oil in a large saucepan. Add the onion and sauté, stirring occasionally, for about 5 minutes. Add the squid and sauté, stirring occasionally, for 5 minutes. Add the tomato purée, 3 of the garlic cloves and the chilli.

3. Season the fish to taste with salt and pepper and add it to the pan. Pour in the white wine and 120 ml/4 fl oz of the fish stock. Transfer the mixture to an ovenproof dish and bake in a preheated oven at 180°C/350°F/Gas 4 for about 10 minutes.

4. Pound together 1 of the remaining garlic cloves, the almonds and crispbread in a mortar. Stir in 30 ml/2 tablespoons each of the remaining olive oil and fish stock. Remove the dish from the oven and add the almond mixture. Stir in the aniseed liqueur. Crush the remaining garlic clove and add it to the dish, together with the rosemary, langoustines and prawns. Arrange the mussels on top.

5. Return the dish to the oven for a further 15 minutes, until the mussels open. Discard any that remain shut. Chop the parsley, sprinkle it over the dish and serve the hotpot immediately.

Above: Barcelona fish hotpot
Below: Fisherman's stew

Basque-style omelette

Piperrada a la vasca

Easy

Serves 4
1 onion
2 green peppers
2 red pepper
2 large tomatoes
45 ml/3 tablespoons olive oil
15 g/½ oz butter
2 cloves garlic
pinch of sugar
50 g/2 oz smoked streaky bacon, rinds removed
115 g/4 oz boiled ham
6 eggs
salt and freshly ground black pepper

- Approximately per portion:
  3,200 kJ/700 kcal
  25 g protein, 36 g fat
  14 g carbohydrate

- Approximate preparation time: 30 minutes

1. Chop the onion. Core, seed and dice the peppers. Briefly blanch the tomatoes. Peel, seed and finely chop the flesh.

2. Heat together the olive oil and butter in a heavy-based frying pan. Add the onion and peppers and sauté over a low heat for about 10 minutes.

3. Finely chop the garlic, then pound it in a mortar together with 2–3 pieces of tomato. Add the remaining tomatoes, together with the garlic mixture to the frying pan. Increase the heat, stir in the sugar and season to taste with salt and pepper.

4. Finely chop the bacon and dry-fry it in another frying pan until the fat runs. Cut the ham into strips, add it to the bacon and cook for about 2 minutes. Remove the pan from the heat.

5. Beat the eggs until they are foamy. Season with a little salt and pepper and pour them over the vegetables. Pour the bacon fat over the omelette. Cook over a low heat until the eggs are just set. Scatter the bacon and ham mixture over the cooked omelette and slide it out of the pan on to a warm serving dish or serve directly from the pan.

Spanish-style potato tortilla

Tortilla de patatas a la española

Good value

Serves 4
4 large potatoes
45–60 ml/3–4 tablespoons olive oil
1 large onion
8 eggs
salt

- Approximately per portion:
  2,000 kJ/480 kcal
  13 g protein, 39 g fat
  17 g carbohydrate

- Approximate preparation time: 40 minutes

1. Peel and dice the potatoes into very small cubes. Heat 30 ml/2 tablespoons of the olive oil in a frying pan. Add the potatoes and sauté over a medium heat for about 5 minutes.

2. Finely chop the onion. Add to the pan, half cover and sauté for about 3 minutes. Remove the pan from the heat, transfer the potato and onion mixture to a bowl and sprinkle a little salt over it.

3. Beat the eggs until they are foamy and mix them with the potatoes. Heat the remaining oil in the frying pan. Pour the egg and potato mixture into the pan. As soon as the eggs begin to set, stir the tortilla a little and form it into an even shape. When the tortilla is lightly fried on the underside, cover the frying pan with a plate and invert it. Slide the tortilla back into the frying pan and finish cooking it. Serve immediately.

Variation

Drain a small can of tuna, mash with a fork and mix it with the potatoes and eggs. Season with pepper, and stir in chopped parsley and grated cheese. Instead of onion, use 2 finely chopped cloves of garlic.

Above: Basque-style omelette
Below: Spanish-style potato tortilla

Macaroni Basque-style

Macarrones a la vasca

Easy

Serves 4

400 g/14 oz dried macaroni
200 g/7 oz Emmenthal cheese
200 g/7 oz butter
freshly ground black pepper

Approximately per portion:

3,800 kJ/900 kcal
28 g protein, 59 g fat
67 g carbohydrate

● Approximate preparation time: 45 minutes

1. Bring a large pan of salted water to the boil. Add the macaroni, stir and bring back to the boil. Lower the heat and simmer for about 10–15 minutes, until it is tender, but still firm to the bite.

2. Grate the cheese. Thoroughly grease an ovenproof dish with a little of the butter.

3. Dice the remaining butter. Spoon the macaroni into the prepared dish, layering it with the butter and cheese. Sprinkle each layer with a little pepper. Finish with a layer of cheese. Bake the macaroni in a preheated oven at 220°C/425°F/Gas 7 for about 15 minutes. Serve immediately.

Baked pasta rolls

Canalones

Rather time-consuming

Serves 4

225 g/8 oz pork fillet
275 g/10 oz veal fillet
115 g/4 oz butter, plus extra
    for greasing
2 onions
200 ml/7 fl oz white wine
30 ml/2 tablespoons ground
    almonds
5 ml/1 teaspoon dried thyme
1 bay leaf, crushed into small pieces
pinch of freshly grated nutmeg
25 g/1 oz plain flour
500 ml/17 fl oz milk
250 g/9 oz lasagne
45 ml/3 tablespoons grated
    Emmenthal cheese
salt and freshly ground black pepper

Approximately per portion:

2,200 kJ/520 kcal
36 g protein, 32 g fat
13 g carbohydrate

● Approximate preparation time: 1 hour

1. Cut the pork and veal into thin strips. Melt 25 g/1 oz of the butter in a frying pan. Add the pork strips and fry, stirring frequently, for about 3 minutes. Remove from the pan and set aside to cool. Chop the onion, add it to the pan and fry until light brown.

2. Finely mince the pork. Add the pork and veal strips to the onions. Mix the pork and veal together

and stir in the wine, almonds, thyme, bay leaf and nutmeg. Season to taste with salt and pepper.

3. Melt 50 g/2 oz of the remaining butter in a saucepan and stir in the flour. Gradually stir in the milk and cook, stirring constantly, until the sauce has thickened.

4. Bring a large saucepan of salted water to the boil. Add the pasta and cook until it is nearly tender. Drain and refresh with cold water. Spread it to dry on a tea towel.

5. Cut the pasta into 10 cm/4 inch long rectangles. Grease an ovenproof dish with butter. Spread out the pasta rectangles. Spoon some of the meat mixture on to each rectangle and roll it up.

6. Arrange the rolls in the prepared dish, seam side down, in a single layer and cover them with the sauce. Sprinkle with grated cheese and dot with the remaining butter. Bake in the middle of a preheated oven at 180°C/350°F/Gas 4 for about 20 minutes, until golden and bubbling. Serve immediately.

Above: Macaroni Basque-style
Below: Baked pasta rolls

Paella

Rather expensive • Exclusive

Serves 6–8

115 g/4 oz lean pork
150 g/5 oz breast of lamb
4 conger eel or monkfish cutlets
6–8 small squid, fresh or frozen
400 g/14 oz mussels
1 red pepper
120 ml/4 fl oz olive oil
1 chicken, divided into 6–8 pieces
115 g/4 oz thin chorizo, morcilla
   or other continental
   cooking sausages
1 large onion
400–450 g/14 oz–1 lb Valencia or
   risotto rice
2 tomatoes
90 g/3½ oz green beans, fresh
   or frozen
90 g/3½ oz peas, fresh or frozen
15 ml/1 tablespoon tomato purée
500–750 ml/17 fl oz–1¼ pints
   water or chicken stock
6 canned artichoke hearts
pinch of saffron
6 langoustines or tiger prawns
salt and freshly ground black pepper

Approximately per portion:

3,300 kJ/790 kcal
67 g protein, 39 g fat
47 g carbohydrate

● Approximate preparation
   time: 1¼ hours

1. Cut the pork and lamb into 2.5 cm/1 inch cubes. Dice the eel or monkfish, discarding any bones.

2. If necessary, clean the squid by pulling the head from the body. Cut off and reserve the tentacles and squeeze out the beak. Pull out the transparent quill from the body, together with any membrane. Rinse and peel off all the skin. Cut the squid into rings.

3. Debeard and scrub the mussels under cold running water. Discard any that do not shut immediately when sharply tapped with the back of a knife. Core and seed the peppers and cut the flesh into thin strips. Heat the olive oil in a paella pan or in 2 large frying pans. Cut 2 cloves of the garlic in half. Add to the pan, fry briefly, then remove them from the pan.

4. Add the chicken pieces, sausages, squid, pork and lamb and fry over a medium heat. Finely chop the onion and remaining garlic and add them to the pan, together with the pepper. Fry for about 5 minutes.

5. Add the rice and cook, stirring constantly, until it is transparent.

6. Briefly blanch the tomatoes, then peel and chop. Mix them into the paella, together with the diced fish and the tomato purée, and cook for about 3 minutes. Add the water or stock, then add the beans, peas and artichoke hearts. Stir in the saffron and season to taste with salt and pepper.

7. Arrange the langoustines or prawns on top of the rice and place the mussels around the sides of the pan. Bring to the boil and cook for about 15 minutes. If necessary, add more seasoning. Do not stir again, but gently shake the pan from time to time. The rice must not overcook, but should be fairly dry.

8. When the paella is cooked, serve it at once straight from the paella pan.

Variations

Paella con caracoles

The paella is prepared as described here, but instead of pork and lamb, use more chicken or rabbit and instead of mussels, use snails. Usually, broad beans are used instead of green beans. The paella is additionally seasoned with fresh rosemary.

Paella campesina

For this recipe from Andalusia. cut the chicken into pieces, then add diced ham and slices of hot chorizo. Cook until half tender, then add the onions and the rice and finish cooking.

Paella del mar

Omit the meat and use only fish, squid, mussels and prawns.

Rice Cuban-style

Arroz a la cubana

Good value

Serves 4

500 g/1 1/4 lb tomatoes
90 ml/6 tablespoons olive oil
pinch of sugar
2 cloves garlic
75 g/3 oz streaky bacon
400 g/14 oz long grain rice
750 ml/1 1/4 pints chicken stock
4 small bananas
6 eggs
30 ml/2 tablespoons plain flour
salt and freshly ground black pepper

- Approximately per portion:
  3,900 kJ/930 kcal
  23 g protein, 48 g fat
  85 g carbohydrate

Approximately per portion:

- Approximate preparation
  time: 45 minutes

1. Blanch the tomatoes. Peel, seed and finely chop the flesh. Heat 15 ml/1 tablespoon of the oil in a saucepan. Add the tomatoes and cook for 5 minutes, until they form a soft purée. Stir in the sugar and season to taste.

2. Finely chop the garlic, together with the bacon. Heat 30 ml/ 2 tablespoons of the remaining oil in a large saucepan. Add the garlic and bacon and fry for 2–3 minutes. Add the rice and cook, stirring constantly, for 3 minutes. Add the stock, season with salt and pepper and cook for about 15 minutes.

3. Peel the bananas. Cut them in half across, then lengthways. Lightly

beat 2 of the eggs. Coat the banana slices in flour and then in beaten egg. Heat 15 ml/1 tablespoon of the remaining oil. Add the banana slices and fry until golden brown. Fry the remaining eggs in the remaining oil. Season to taste.

4. Drain the rice and arrange it on warm individual plates. Pour the sauce on top and serve with the fried eggs and bananas.

Black rice

Arroz negro

Exquisite

Serves 4

400 g/14 oz small squid, with ink sacs
3 large tomatoes
1 red or 1 green pepper
45 ml/3 tablespoons olive oil
2 large onions
1 clove garlic
350 g/12 oz Valencia or round grain rice
750 ml/1 1/4 pints hot water or vegetable stock
15–30 ml/1–2 tablespoons dry sherry
salt and freshly ground black pepper

Approximately per portion:

- 2,200 kJ/520 kcal
  23 g protein, 17 g fat
  77 g carbohydrate

- Approximate preparation
  time: 50 minutes

1. Clean the squid by pulling the head from the body. Cut off the tentacles and squeeze out the beak.

Pull the quill from the body and remove any membrane. Carefully remove the ink sacs and keep in a bowl of water until required. Wash the squid bodies and remove the skin. Cut the larger ones in half.

2. Briefly blanch the tomatoes. Peel, seed and finely chop the flesh. Peel, seed and dice the pepper. Heat the olive oil in a large saucepan. Chop the onion. Add the onion and pepper to the pan and sauté for about 3 minutes.

3. Add the squid. Crush the garlic and add it to the pan, together with the tomatoes. Cover and cook over a low heat for about 10 minutes, until thickened. Add the rice and stir well. Pour in the water or vegetable stock. Preheat the oven to 200°C/400°F/Gas 6.

4. Remove the ink sacs from the water and cut them open over a small bowl. Add enough ink to the rice to make it turn black. Cook the rice for a further 15 minutes. Season well with salt and pepper and add the sherry.

5. Transfer the rice mixture to an ovenproof dish and let it dry out in the switched off oven for about 10 minutes. Serve immediately.

Above: Rice Cuban-style
Below: Black rice

Sea bream Madrid-style

Besugo a la madrileña

For guests • Fairly easy

Serves 4

1 cleaned sea bream, about
800 g–1 kg/1³/4–2¹/4 lb
60 ml/4 tablespoons olive oil
1 bunch parsley
2 onions
30 ml/2 tablespoons breadcrumbs
2 cloves garlic
1 clove
120 ml/4 fl oz white wine
¹/2 lemon
salt and freshly ground black pepper

Approximately per portion:
1,900 kJ/450 kcal
39 g protein, 22 g fat
15 g carbohydrate

● Approximate preparation
time: 40 minutes

1. Season the fish with salt and pepper inside and out and make about 6 diagonal cuts into the skin on both sides. Pour 30 ml/ 2 tablespoons of the olive oil into an ovenproof dish and place the fish in it. Add enough water to come halfway up the fish.

2. Chop the parsley. Chop the onions. Mix together the breadcrumbs, the parsley and onions. Crush the garlic and add it to the mixture.

3. Heat the remaining olive oil in a small frying pan, together with the clove. Remove the clove and add the oil to the onion mixture. Stir in the wine and season to taste with salt and pepper. Cut the lemon into thin slices.

4. Bake the fish in a preheated oven at 180°C/350°F/Gas 4 for about 10 minutes.

5. Remove the dish from the oven and insert the lemon slices into the cuts in the fish. Pour the sauce over it and bake for a further 15 minutes. Serve immediately.

Gilt-headed bream in a salt crust

Dorada al la sal

Quick

Serves 4

2 kg/4¹/2 lb coarse sea salt
1 gilt-headed bream, about
800 g–1 kg/1³/4–2¹/4 lb, cleaned
but not scaled
15–30 ml/1–2 tablespoons water
To serve:
juice of 1 lemon
30 ml/2 tablespoons olive oil
freshly ground black pepper

Approximately per portion:
1,400 kJ/290 kcal
36 g protein, 11 g fat
3 g carbohydrate

● Approximate preparation
time: 30 minutes

1. Put a 2.5 cm/1 inch layer of salt on the base of a large, oval non-metallic dish. Rinse the fish in cold water; pat it dry with kitchen paper and place it on the salt. Spread the remaining salt over the top and press it in well. Sprinkle it with the water.

2. Cover the dish and bake the fish in a preheated oven at 240°C/ 475°F/Gas 9 for about 20 minutes. Remove the dish from the oven and set aside for 5 minutes.

3. Remove the salt crust from all around the fish with a pointed knife and transfer the fish to a serving dish.

4. At the table, remove the skin, remove the top fillet from the backbone and divide it into portions. Then remove the backbone and take out the bottom fillet. Remove its skin and similarly divide the fillet into portions. Sprinkle the fish pieces with the oil and lemon juice and grind pepper on to it straight from the pepper mill.

Tip

Gilt-headed bream is sometimes sold under its French name daurade. Note that this is not the same as dorade, which is red sea bream. However, they are equally delicious and this recipe could also be made with any type of sea bream.

Above: Sea bream Madrid-style
Below: Gilt-headed bream in a salt crust

Hake with green sauce

Merluza a la vasca

Exquisite

Serves 4

4 hake steaks
15 ml/1 tablespoon plain flour
1 large onion
2 large cloves garlic
200 g/7 oz mussels
60 ml/4 tablespoons olive oil
120 ml/4 fl oz water
60 ml/4 tablespoons white wine
150 g/5 oz green peas, fresh or frozen
8 asparagus tips, fresh or canned
15 ml/1 tablespoon lemon juice
1 bunch parsley
salt and freshly ground black pepper

Approximately per portion:

• 1,800 kJ/430 kcal
38 g protein, 22 g fat
14 g carbohydrate

• Approximate preparation time: 40 minutes

Tip

It is very important to throw away any mussels with damaged shells and any that do not open during cooking.

1. Rub the fish all over with a little salt and pepper and coat in the flour. Chop the onion and garlic. Debeard and scrub the mussels under cold running water. Discard any that do not shut immediately when sharply tapped with the back of a knife.

2. Put them in a saucepan with the water, cover and bring to the boil. Cook, shaking the pan from time to time, until the shells open. Heat the oil in a frying pan. Add the onion and garlic and sauté until soft and translucent. Add the fish and cook over a low heat for about 8 minutes.

3. Remove the fish from the pan. Drain the mussels, reserving the cooking liquid. Discard any that have not opened. Strain the cooking liquid and add to the onions, together with the wine. Cook for about 3 minutes, add the peas and cook for a further 5 minutes. Add the asparagus tips, cover and cook over a low heat for about 5 minutes.

4. Remove the peas and asparagus tips, arrange them with the fish and mussels and keep warm. Season the sauce to taste with salt and pepper and beat in the lemon juice with a whisk. Chop the parsley and sprinkle it over the fish. Serve immediately with the sauce.

Trout Pyrenean-style

Truchas al estilo del Pirineo

Quick

Serves 4

1 red pepper
90 ml/6 tablespoons olive oil
200 g/7 oz bacon, rinds removed
1 small fresh red chilli
4 cleaned trout, each about
*   250 g/9 oz*
1 clove garlic
30 ml/2 tablespoons white
*   wine vinegar*
salt and freshly ground black pepper

Approximately per portion:

3,100 kJ/740 kcal
58 g protein, 54 g fat
4 g carbohydrate

● Approximate preparation
  time: 30 minutes

Variation

In the Navarre region, the trout
are stuffed with a slice of raw ham,
seasoned with salt and pepper,
coated in flour and fried in olive oil
for about 10 minutes on each side.

1. Core, seed and dice the red
pepper. Heat 15 ml/1 tablespoon
of the oil in a frying pan. Add the
pepper and sauté over a medium
heat for about 10 minutes.
Remove the pan from the heat
and set aside to cool.

2. Finely chop the bacon and chilli
and add to the red pepper, mixing
well. If you prefer a milder taste,
seed the chilli before chopping it.

3. Stuff the trout with the pepper
and bacon mixture. Pour 15 ml/
1 tablespoon of the remaining
olive oil into an ovenproof dish.
Season the fish with salt and
pepper and arrange them in the
dish. Place the garlic cloves beside
the trout and pour over the
remaining olive oil. Cook in a
preheated oven at 220°C/425°F/
Gas 7 for about 12 minutes.

4. Arrange the trout on individual
serving plates and keep warm. Add
the vinegar to the cooking liquid, if
necessary season with a little salt
and pour this sauce over the trout.
Serve immediately.

Monkfish fisherman-style

Rape a la marinera

Easy

Serves 4

1 onion
3 cloves garlic
1 carrot
300 g/11 oz fish trimmings, bones or heads
300 ml/1/2 pint water
4 monkfish steaks, skinned and boned
juice of 1/2 lemon
15 ml/1 tablespoon plain flour
30 ml/2 tablespoons olive oil
500 g/1 1/4 lb peeled tomatoes, fresh or canned
200 g/7 oz peas, fresh or frozen
15 ml/1 tablespoon chopped fresh mixed herbs, such as thyme, rosemary and marjoram
2.5 ml/1/2 teaspoon mild paprika
50 ml/2 fl oz wine
pinch of sugar
pinch of saffron
1/2 bunch parsley
salt and freshly ground white pepper

Approximately per portion:
1,600 kJ/380 kcal
43 g protein, 12 g fat
21 g carbohydrate

● Approximate preparation time: 50 minutes

---

1. Peel the onion and 1 garlic clove, then put them, together with the carrot and fish trimmings, bones or heads in a large saucepan and add the water. Bring to the boil, cover and simmer over a medium heat for about 15 minutes.

2. Sprinkle the fish steaks with lemon juice, cover and marinate in the refrigerator for about 10 minutes. Pat them dry with kitchen paper and sprinkle with flour. Heat the olive oil in a large frying pan. Add the fish and fry over a medium heat for about 5 minutes on each side.

3. Add the tomatoes, peas, herbs and paprika and fry for about 5 minutes. Strain the fish stock and add 90 ml/6 tablespoons to the pan, together with the wine. Cook over a low heat for 5 minutes. Stir in the sugar and saffron and season to taste with salt and pepper.

4. Chop the parsley and crush the remaining garlic. Transfer the fish and vegetables to a warm serving dish, sprinkle with the parsley and garlic and serve immediately.

Baked fish

Pescado al horno

For guests

Serves 4

400 g/14 oz potatoes
800 g/1 3/4 lb sea bass or sea bream
120 ml/4 fl oz olive oil
200 ml/7 fl oz dry sherry
2 lemons
500 g/1 1/4 lb small tomatoes
2 large onions
1 bunch parsley
salt and freshly ground black pepper

Approximately per portion:
2,500 kJ/600 kcal
37 g protein, 35 g fat
24 g carbohydrate

● Approximate preparation time: 45 minutes

---

1. Peel the potatoes and cut into thin slices. Cook them in a small quantity of boiling water for about 10 minutes.

2. Season the fish with a little salt and pepper and put it into an ovenproof dish, together with 60 ml/4 tablespoons of the olive oil. Bake in a preheated oven at 200°C/400°F/Gas 6 for about 10 minutes.

3. Pour the sherry over the fish and add the potatoes. Thinly slice the lemons and add them to the fish. Bake for a further 10 minutes.

4. Briefly blanch the tomatoes. Peel and cut them in half. Heat 15 ml/1 tablespoon of the remaining olive oil. Add the tomatoes and cook for about 3 minutes. Slice the onions. Heat the remaining olive oil and sauté the onions until they are soft and translucent. Chop the parsley.

5. When the fish and potatoes are tender, remove the dish from the oven and garnish with the onions, tomatoes and parsley. Serve immediately straight from the dish.

Above: Monkfish fisherman-style
Below: Baked fish

Fried squid

Calamares a la romana

Fresh squid tastes best, but you can use frozen if necessary. You could also use cuttlefish.

Easy

Serves 4
150 g/5 oz plain flour
250 ml/8 fl oz dry white wine
5 ml/1 teaspoon salt
2 large prepared squid
1 egg white
juice of 1 lemon
salt and freshly ground black pepper
oil, for frying
lemon slices and parsley sprigs, to garnish
garlic mayonnaise, to serve (optional)

1. Put the flour, white wine and a pinch of salt into a bowl and beat with the whisk until smooth. Cover the bowl and set aside for about 2 hours.

2. Meanwhile, cut the squid into rings. Sprinkle them with the lemon juice and season with a little salt and pepper. Cover and set aside in the refrigerator for about 2 hours.

3. Beat the egg white until stiff peaks form, then carefully fold it into the batter.

4. Heat the oil in a deep-fat fryer. Remove the squid from the marinade and drain thoroughly. Coat the squid rings in batter and drain off any excess. Fry them for about 3 minutes, until they are crisp and golden. Drain well and garnish with lemon slices and parsley sprigs. Serve with garlic mayonnaise, if liked.

Small grilled squid

Pulpitos a la plancha

Quick

Serves 4
30 ml/2 tablespoons olive oil
400 g/14 oz prepared small squid
1 bunch parsley
4 cloves garlic
15 ml/1 tablespoon lemon juice
salt and freshly ground black pepper

1. Brush the grill pan with a little of the olive oil and preheat. Arrange the squid on it and grill for about 5 minutes, until they begin to colour. Turn them over from time to time and brush with the remaining oil.

2. Chop the parsley and garlic and mix them together.

3. As soon as the squid are light golden brown, remove them from the grill and arrange them on plates. Sprinkle with lemon juice and season well with salt and pepper. Finally, sprinkle the parsley and garlic mixture on top and serve immediately.

This recipe is also superb made with small octopus, but these can be difficult to obtain. If you do see them, buy them as they have firm, sweet flesh. If they have not already been tenderized, put them in a plastic bag and beat thoroughly with a meat mallet or rolling pin.

Above: Fried squid
Below: Small grilled squid

Mussels Catalan-style

Mejillones a la catalana

Quick

Serves 4

2 kg/4¹/₂ lb mussels
I large onion
4 cloves garlic
105 ml/7 tablespoons olive oil
4 tomatoes
¹/₂ bay leaf
15 ml/I tablespoon brandy
2.5 ml/¹/₂ teaspoon mild paprika
salt and freshly ground
   black pepper

Approximately per portion:
2,300 kJ/550 kcal
51 g protein, 32 g fat
10 g carbohydrate

● Approximate preparation
   time: 25 minutes

1. Debeard and scrub the mussels under cold running water. Discard any that do not shut immediately when sharply tapped with the back of a knife.

2. Finely chop the onion and garlic. Heat the olive oil in a large, heavy-based frying pan. Add the onion and garlic and sauté over a medium heat, stirring occasionally, for about 3 minutes, or until the onion is soft and translucent.

3. Briefly blanch the tomatoes in boiling water. Peel, seed and finely chop the flesh. Add the tomatoes to the frying pan, together with the bay leaf, and fry for about

5 minutes. Add the brandy and paprika and season to taste with a little salt and pepper.

4. Add the mussels, cover and cook over a high heat, shaking the pan from time to time, until the shells open. Discard any mussels that do not open. Arrange the mussels on a serving plate, pour over the sauce and set aside to cool before serving.

Shellfish with yellow sauce

Almejas con salsa amarilla

For guests

Serves 4

2 kg/4¹/₂ lb shellfish, such as
   mussels or clams
45 ml/3 tablespoons olive oil
I large onion
250 ml/8 fl oz dry white wine
I bunch parsley
pinch of saffron
6 cloves garlic
2.5 ml/¹/₂ teaspoon turmeric
salt and freshly ground black pepper

Approximately per portion:
2,300 kJ/600 kcal
32 g protein, 16 g fat
17 g carbohydrate

● Approximate preparation
   time: 3 hours of which
   2¹/₂ hours are soaking time

1. Soak the shellfish for about 2¹/₂ hours in a large container of cold water, changing the water several times. Drain well.

2. Heat the olive oil in a large saucepan. Chop the onion, add to the pan and sauté for about 3 minutes. Add the shellfish and wine and season to taste with a little salt and plenty of pepper. Cover and cook over a high heat until the shells open. Meanwhile, chop the parsley. Remove the shellfish from the pan. Strain and reserve the cooking liquid.

3. Pound together the turmeric, saffron, parsley and garlic in a mortar with a pestle. Add the shellfish and heat through, but do not boil again. Transfer to a warm serving dish and serve immediately.

4. Stir in the spice paste and season to taste with salt and pepper. Add the shellfish and heat through, but do not boil again. Transfer to a warm serving dish and serve immediately.

Above: Mussels Catalan-style
Below: Shellfish with yellow sauce

MEAT AND POULTRY DISHES

Leg of lamb Castillian-style

Pierna de cordero asado a la castellana

For guests

Serves 6

2 cloves garlic
15 ml/1 tablespoon olive oil
50 g/2 oz butter
15 ml/1 tablespoon mild paprika
2.5 ml/½ teaspoon caraway seeds
2.5 ml/½ teaspoon dried oregano
5 ml/1 teaspoon dried rosemary
1 leg of lamb, about 1.5 kg/ 3–3½ lb
1 onion
1 bay leaf
120 ml/4 fl oz dry white wine
250 ml/8 fl oz water
3 lemons
salt and freshly ground black pepper
fresh herb sprigs, to garnish

- Approximate preparation time: 1 hour

Approximately per portion:
2,900 kJ/690 kcal
46 g protein, 55 g fat
3 g carbohydrate

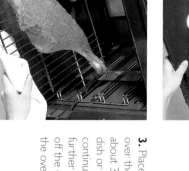

1. Crush the garlic. Mix together the olive oil, butter, garlic, paprika, caraway seeds, oregano and rosemary and season to taste with salt and pepper. Rub this paste all over the leg of lamb.

2. Put the onion into an ovenproof dish or on a baking tray, together with the bay leaf, wine and water. Put the dish or tray into the bottom of a preheated oven at 240°C/475°F/Gas 9.

3. Place the leg of lamb on a rack over the dish or tin and cook for about 30 minutes. Remove the dish or tin from the oven and continue to roast the lamb for a further 10 minutes. Then switch off the oven and leave the lamb in the oven for a further 10 minutes.

4. Meanwhile, put the cooking juices in a saucepan and bring to the boil. Lower the heat and simmer for 10 minutes. Carve the lamb and transfer to a serving dish. Strain the sauce over it. Slice the lemons and use to garnish the lamb, together with fresh herb sprigs. Serve immediately.

Tip

This recipe is even more successful if you cook the leg of lamb on a rotating spit. The exact roasting time depends on the size of the leg of lamb. It is best to use a meat thermometer to check that it is cooked through.

Veal with peppers

Estufado de ternera con pimientos

Rather time-consuming

Serves 4

1 large aubergine
600 g/1 lb 5 oz boneless veal
45 ml/3 tablespoons olive oil
1 large onion
1 red pepper
1 green pepper
30 ml/2 tablespoons tomato purée
5 ml/1 teaspoon chopped thyme
5 ml/1 teaspoon chopped rosemary
5 ml/1 teaspoon chopped marjoram
1 bay leaf
250 ml/8 fl oz red wine
3 cloves garlic
115 g/4 oz calf's or lamb's liver
pinch of saffron
15 ml/1 tablespoon shelled almonds
1 small fresh red chilli
45 ml/3 tablespoons chicken stock
400 g/14 oz new potatoes
salt and freshly ground black pepper

Approximately per portion:
1,600 kJ/380 kcal
42 g protein, 6 g fat
27 g carbohydrate

● Approximate preparation
time: 2 hours

1. Peel the aubergine and cut it into 1 cm/½ inch thick slices. Put it in a colander; sprinkle with salt and set aside for about 10 minutes. Rinse, pat dry with kitchen paper and dice. Dice the veal into 2.5 cm/1 inch cubes. Heat the oil in a large frying pan. Add the aubergine and the veal and fry, stirring frequently, for about 15 minutes.

2. Chop the onion. Core and seed the peppers and cut the flesh into strips. Add the onion, peppers and tomato purée to the pan. Stir in the herbs and cook for about 5 minutes. Pour in the wine.

3. Transfer the mixture to an ovenproof dish, season to taste with salt and pepper and bake in a preheated oven at 160°C/325°F/ Gas 3 for about 40 minutes. Coarsely chop the garlic. Chop the liver. Put the garlic, liver, saffron, almonds and chilli in a food processor and process to a soft paste. For a milder flavour, seed the chilli first. Add a little stock.

4. Cut the potatoes in half, add them to the veal and bake for 20 minutes. Add the liver mixture to the veal and bake for a further 10 minutes. Transfer the meat and potatoes to a warm serving dish and keep warm. If necessary, re-heat the sauce, then pour it over the meat and potatoes. Serve immediately.

Rice with rabbit

Arroz con conejo

Rabbit is popular and inexpensive in Spain and similar dishes are served at family meals all over the country at least once a week. Most fresh rabbit on sale has been farmed. Domesticated rabbit has light-coloured, delicately-flavoured flesh. Wild rabbit meat is darker and less widely available. Most frozen rabbit is imported and lacks the flavour of fresh rabbit. It may also have a tendency to dry out during cooking.

Easy

Serves 4

675 g/1 ½ lb boneless rabbit
60 ml/4 tablespoons olive oil
200 g/7 oz smoked streaky bacon, rinds removed
2 large onions
400 g/14 oz Valencia or round grain rice
1 litre/1 ¾ pints beef stock
150 g/5 oz pimientos in brine or 2 small red peppers
200 g/7 oz peas, fresh or frozen
salt and freshly ground black pepper

Approximately per portion:
5,900 kJ/1,400 kcal
89 g protein, 81 g fat
68 g carbohydrate

● Approximate preparation time: 1 hour

44

1. Cut the rabbit into 2.5 cm/ 1 inch cubes. Heat a paella pan or

large heavy-based frying pan and then add the olive oil. When the oil is hot, add the rabbit and fry over a medium heat, stirring and turning frequently, for about 10 minutes.

2. Finely dice the bacon and dry-fry it in a separate frying pan until it is crisp and has rendered all its fat. Remove the bacon and rabbit from the frying pans and set aside.

3. Add the bacon fat to the oil in which the rabbit was fried. Finely chop the onions. Add them to the pan and fry, stirring frequently, until they are golden.

4. Add the rice to the pan, stir well and pour in about 750 ml/ 1¼ pints of the beef stock. Bring to the boil, then add the rabbit meat and the bacon.

5. Cook the rabbit and rice over a low heat, stirring occasionally, for about 20 minutes. If necessary, add some of the remaining stock.

6. Drain the bottled pimientos and cut them into thin strips, if using. Core and seed the fresh peppers and cut the flesh into strips, if using. Mix the pimientos or peppers and peas with the rabbit rice. Season to taste with salt and pepper.

7. Transfer the paella pan to a preheated oven at 240°C/475°F/ Gas 9 for 5 minutes. Serve immediately straight from the pan. If you have not used an ovenproof pan or one with an ovenproof handle, transfer the rabbit rice to an ovenproof dish before putting it into the oven.

Variation

The ingredients of this dish vary according to the region – and the available produce. Often, instead of peas, green beans are used and 1–2 finely chopped tomatoes are added as well. With this variation, the rice is also seasoned with a pinch of saffron.

Tip

Strictly speaking, a paella is a pan, from which the well-known dish took its name (see page 28). It used for cooking a variety of rice-based dishes. Traditionally, it is made of heavy cast iron with handles on either side. This type must be properly seasoned before use. Paellas made from other materials are also available from good kitchenware shops. However, make sure that whatever type you buy has a heavy base to prevent the rice from scorching.

Spaniards are particularly partial to rabbit dishes.

Roast chicken with vegetables

Pollo en xanfaina

Easy

Serves 4

1 roasting chicken, about 1 kg/ 2 1/4 lb
90 ml/6 tablespoons olive oil
400 g/14 oz aubergines
300 g/11 oz small courgettes
3 large onions
4 large tomatoes
2 cloves garlic
1 bay leaf
2 slices white bread
105 ml/7 tablespoons sherry
salt and freshly ground black pepper

Approximately per portion:
3,000 kJ/710 kcal
57 g protein, 45 g fat
19 g carbohydrate

● Approximate preparation time: 1 hour

---

1. Divide the chicken into 8 pieces. Heat 30 ml/2 tablespoons of the olive oil in a large frying pan. Add the chicken pieces and fry for about 5 minutes. Remove the chicken pieces from the pan and sprinkle them with salt and pepper.

2. Cut the aubergines and courgettes into 1 cm/1/2 inch cubes. Dice the onions. Briefly blanch the tomatoes. Peel, seed and finely chop the flesh.

3. Add 30 ml/2 tablespoons of the remaining olive oil to the frying pan. Add the diced aubergines, courgettes, onions and tomatoes. Chop the garlic and add it to the pan, together with the bay leaf. Season to taste with salt and pepper and fry the vegetables for about 10 minutes.

4. Put the chicken into an ovenproof dish, add the vegetables and pour in the sherry. Cover the dish with foil.

5. Bake the chicken in a preheated oven at 180°C/350°F/Gas 4 for about 10 minutes. Remove the foil and continue to bake the chicken for a further 20 minutes, until cooked through.

6. Meanwhile, cut the bread into 4 triangles. Heat the remaining oil and fry the bread triangles on both sides until golden. Garnish the chicken with the fried bread triangles and serve immediately.

Chicken with almond sauce

Gallina en pepitoria

Exquisite

Serves 4

2 eggs
1.5 kg/3–3 1/2 lb roasting chicken
1 large onion
4 cloves garlic
115 g/4 oz raw ham
90 ml/6 tablespoons olive oil
1 slice day-old white bread
12 shelled almonds
5 ml/1 teaspoon lemon juice
500 ml/17 fl oz chicken stock
pinch of saffron
pinch of ground cloves
1 bay leaf
salt and freshly ground black pepper

Approximately per portion:
4,100 kJ/980 kcal
88 g protein, 65 g fat
11 g carbohydrate

● Approximate preparation time: 1 hour

---

1. Hard-boil the eggs. Put them in cold water, then peel them. Divide the chicken into 8 pieces. Chop the onion and garlic. Dice the ham.

2. Heat the olive oil in a frying pan and fry the bread, almonds and one quarter of the garlic until they are golden. Remove them all from the frying pan and drain. Add the onion to the pan and sauté for about 3 minutes. Add the chicken and ham and pour in the lemon juice and stock. Stir in the ground cloves, add the bay leaf and season with salt and pepper. Cook over a low heat for about 25 minutes.

3. Pound together the bread, almonds and the remaining garlic in a mortar. Add the saffron. Cut the eggs in half, rub the yolks through a strainer and add to the mixture. Stir in 15–30 ml/1–2 tablespoons of the stock to make a paste.

4. Remove the chicken from the pan. Bring the liquid to the boil and cook until reduced by about one third. Remove and discard the bay leaf. Stir in the almond paste and season to taste with salt and pepper. Return the pieces of chicken to the pan to heat through. Serve immediately.

Above: Roast chicken with vegetables
Below: Chicken with almond sauce

Chicken with crayfish

Pollo con langosta

This unusual and rather daring combination is not nouvelle cuisine. It is a thoroughly traditional recipe from the Spanish Mediterranean coast. The slightly sweet flavour of the crayfish goes very well with the chicken and the delicious spicy sauce.

Exquisite

Serves 4

1 kg/2¼ lb chicken
50 g/2 oz smoked streaky bacon, rinds removed
2 cooked, peeled crayfish tails, fresh or frozen
4 tomatoes
2 onions
30 ml/2 tablespoons olive oil
8 cloves garlic
120 ml/4 fl oz dry white wine
pinch of ground cinnamon
pinch of saffron
1 sprig celery leaves
5 ml/1 teaspoon fresh rosemary
45 ml/3 tablespoons brandy
8 shelled almonds
115 g/4 oz chicken liver
10 g/¼ oz plain chocolate
salt and freshly ground black pepper

Approximately per portion:
2,900 kJ/690 kcal
65 g protein, 40 g fat
10 g carbohydrate

● Approximate preparation time: 1 hour 10 minutes

1. Divide the chicken into 8 pieces. To do this, first cut the chicken in half with a sharp knife. Separate the wings and legs from the body, then separate the thighs from the drumsticks. Dice the bacon.

2. Cut the crayfish tails into pieces. Blanch the tomatoes in boiling water and peel them. Finely chop the onions. Heat the oil in a large frying pan. Add the chicken pieces and fry over a medium heat on all sides for about 5 minutes. Then remove them from the frying pan.

3. Add 4 of the garlic cloves and the crayfish pieces to the frying pan and fry for about 3 minutes. Remove the crayfish pieces and garlic and set aside.

4. Add the tomatoes, onions and bacon to the pan and fry for about 5 minutes. Add the chicken pieces, white wine, cinnamon, saffron, celery leaves and rosemary and season to taste with salt and pepper. Cover and cook for about 15 minutes. Add the crayfish pieces and brandy and cook for a further 10 minutes.

Variation:

Instead of crayfish tails, you could use langoustines or lobster.

5. Meanwhile, pound together the almonds, the 4 fried and 4 raw cloves garlic, the chicken liver and the chocolate in a mortar to form a dark paste. Alternatively, process in a food processor with a little of the chicken cooking liquid.

6. Remove the chicken and crayfish from the frying pan. Arrange them on a serving dish and keep warm.

7. Bring the cooking liquid to the boil over a high heat. Add the almond paste, stir well and simmer for about 3 minutes.

8. Season the sauce to taste with a little salt and pepper and pour it over the chicken and crayfish. Serve at once.

Pigs' trotters with pine nuts

Pies de cerdo con piñones

Rather time-consuming

Serves 4

2 onions
1 bay leaf
6 pigs' trotters
500 ml/17 fl oz water
2 eggs
30 ml/2 tablespoons plain flour
25 g/1 oz butter
60 ml/4 tablespoons olive oil
50 g/2 oz pine nuts
500 g/1 1/4 lb tomatoes
30 ml/2 tablespoons tomato purée
200 ml/7 fl oz beef stock
2 cloves garlic
5 almonds
pinch of saffron
15 ml/1 tablespoon breadcrumbs
salt and freshly ground black pepper

Approximately per portion:
3,100 kJ/740 kcal
21 g protein, 59 g fat
30 g carbohydrate

● Approximate preparation
time: 2 1/2 hours

---

1. Stud 1 onion with the bay leaf.
Put the onion, pigs' trotters and
water in a large saucepan, bring to
the boil and simmer for about
45 minutes.

2. Drain and reserve the cooking
liquid. Using a sharp knife, slit the
pigs' trotters and remove the main
bones. Lightly beat the eggs. Coat
the pigs' trotters first in flour and
then in beaten egg.

3. Heat the butter and 45 ml/
3 tablespoons of the oil. Add the
pigs' trotters and fry for about
5 minutes. Add the pine nuts.

4. Blanch and peel the tomatoes.
Chop the remaining onion. Add the
tomatoes and onion to the pan and
cook over a low heat for 5 minutes.
Stir in the tomato purée. Reserve
45 ml/3 tablespoons of the stock
and add the rest to the pan. Season
to taste. Crush the garlic and add it
to the pan. Transfer the mixture to
an ovenproof dish, cover and cook
in a preheated oven at 190°C/
375°F/Gas 5 for about 1 1/4 hours.

5. Grate the almonds. Mix them
with the saffron, breadcrumbs and
olive oil. Stir in the remaining stock.
Pour over the pigs' trotters and
bake for 5 minutes. Serve at once. .

Tripe Madrid-style

Callos a la madrileña

Rather time-consuming

Serves 6

400 g/14 oz pre-cooked tripe
400 g/14 oz calf's feet
400 g/14 oz calf's head
250 ml/8 fl oz dry white wine
1 bay leaf
6 peppercorns, crushed
1 clove
50 g/2 oz raw ham
3 large onions
300 g/11 oz leek
3 carrots
45 ml/3 tablespoons olive oil
5 ml/1 teaspoon paprika
250 g/9 oz can tomatoes
200 g/7 oz chorizo
salt

Approximately per portion:
2,200 kJ/520 kcal
31 g protein, 42 g fat
8 g carbohydrate

● Approximate preparation
time: 3 hours

---

1. Cut the tripe into 1 cm/1/2 inch
wide strips. Cook the calf's feet
and head in boiling salted water for
about 30 minutes.

2. Drain and cut up the feet and
remove the bones. Cut the calf's
head and feet into strips.

3. Put the meat into a flameproof
casserole, together with the wine
and add enough water to cover.
Add a little salt, the bay leaf, the
peppercorns and the clove. Cook
over a low heat for about 1 hour.

4. Cut the ham into strips. Chop
the onions. Finely chop the leek
and carrots. Heat the oil in a frying
pan. Add the ham and fry for
2–3 minutes. Add the onions and
briefly fry them with the ham. Add
the leek and carrots and fry briefly.
Season to taste with salt, cover and
cook for about 5 minutes.

5. Add the vegetables to the
casserole, together with the
tomatoes and their can juice. Slice
the chorizo and add to the
casserole. Bake in a preheated
oven at 190°C/375°F/ Gas 5 for
about 1 hour. Serve immediately.

Above: Pigs' trotters with pine nuts
Below: Tripe Madrid-style

Aubergines with cheese

Berenjenas con queso

Exquisite

Serves 4

6 medium aubergines
1 large onion
60 ml/4 tablespoons olive oil
3 eggs
45–60 ml/3–4 tablespoons breadcrumbs
50 g/2 oz grated goat's cheese
pinch of freshly grated nutmeg
pinch of ground cinnamon
oil, for frying
salt and freshly ground black pepper
cherry tomatoes, to serve

Approximately per portion:
1,400 kJ/330 kcal
10 g protein, 28 g fat
10 g carbohydrate

• Approximate preparation time: 1 hour

1. Peel the aubergines, cut them in half lengthways and cook them in boiling salted water for about 10 minutes.

2. Remove 4 of the aubergine halves and scoop out the flesh to leave shells. Finely chop the flesh. Remove the remaining aubergine halves and chop finely.

3. Chop the onion. Heat the oil in a frying pan. Add the onion and sauté until soft and translucent. Add the chopped aubergine and fry for about 10 minute, until soft. Remove the pan from the heat.

4. Beat 1 egg and mix it with the aubergine mixture. Stir in the breadcrumbs and cheese and season to taste with salt and pepper. Fill the aubergine halves with the mixture. Beat the remaining eggs. Dip the aubergine halves in the egg, then coat them with flour. Heat sufficient oil in a frying pan and fry the aubergines for about 5 minutes. Serve immediately with cherry tomatoes.

Aubergine moulds

Pastel de berenjenas

Exquisite

Serves 4

65 g/2 1/2 oz crispbread
2 red peppers
500 g/1 1/4 lb aubergines
1 tomato
2 onions
45 ml/3 tablespoons olive oil, plus extra for greasing
2 egg yolks
90 ml/6 tablespoons milk
pinch of ground cinnamon
salt and freshly ground black pepper
tomato sauce, to serve

Approximately per portion:
1,200 kJ/290 kcal
6 g protein, 20 g fat
20 g carbohydrate

• Approximate preparation time: 1 3/4 hours

1. Pound the crispbread in a mortar. Core, seed and dice the peppers. Cut the aubergines in half. Scoop out the flesh, leaving the skins intact. Dice the flesh. Blanch the tomatoes, peel and chop the flesh. Chop the onions.

2. Heat the oil in a frying pan. Add the onions and sauté until soft. Add the aubergine flesh and sauté for about 3 minutes, then add the peppers and tomatoes. Season to taste, lower the heat and cook for about 20 minutes, until the vegetables are soft.

3. Remove from the heat and set aside to cool slightly. Transfer to a food processor and process to a purée. Mix the egg yolks with the milk and stir into the purée. Stir in the cinnamon.

4. Brush small moulds or cups with oil. Sprinkle in some of the crispbread crumbs and shake the moulds so that their sides are covered. Mix about three quarters of the remaining crumbs into the vegetable purée.

5. Line the moulds with the aubergine skins. Let these protrude slightly and brush them with a little oil. Spoon the purée into the moulds and sprinkle with the remaining crumbs. Fold the skins over the filling. Put the moulds into a roasting tin. Add sufficient water to come halfway up the sides of the moulds. Cook in a preheated oven at 180°C/350°F/Gas 4 for about 25 minutes. Then leave them to stand in the water for a further 3 minutes. Turn out the moulds on to serving plates. Serve with tomato sauce.

Above: Aubergines with cheese
Below: Aubergine moulds

Spinach with raisins and pine nuts

Espinacas con pasas y piñones

This exquisite side dish comes from Barcelona.

Easy

Serves 4

30 ml/2 tablespoons small raisins or sultanas
115g/4 oz raw ham
800 g/1³/₄ lb young leaf spinach
45 ml/3 tablespoons olive oil
15–30 ml/1–2 tablespoons pine nuts
salt and freshly ground black pepper

1. Put the raisins or sultanas in a small bowl and add sufficient lukewarm water to cover. Set aside to soak for about 1½ hours.

2. Finely dice the ham. Remove the stalks from the spinach. Put the spinach in a large saucepan with just the water clinging to the leaves after washing and sprinkle with a little salt. Cover and bring to the boil over a low heat. Cook for

about 3 minutes, drain and squeeze out the excess moisture.

3. Heat the olive oil in a large frying pan. Add the ham and fry briefly over a low heat, stirring frequently. Add the spinach and cook until all the liquid has evaporated. Drain the raisins well and add them to the pan, together with the pine nuts. Mix thoroughly and season to taste with salt and pepper. Serve immediately.

Beans and peas Mallorca-style

Verdura con huevos a la mallorquina

Exquisite

Serves 4

250 g/9 oz large green beans
1 large onion
2 small potatoes
30 ml/2 tablespoons olive oil
6 slices Spanish chorizo
1 clove garlic
250 ml/8 fl oz stock
250g/9 oz peas, fresh or frozen
4 eggs
pinch of ground cinnamon
pinch of ground cloves
salt and freshly ground black pepper

1. Cut the beans crossways into 2.5 cm/1 inch long pieces. Chop the onion. Peel the potatoes and cut them in 5 mm/¼ inch chunks.

2. Heat the olive oil in a large saucepan. Add the onion and chorizo and fry over a medium heat for about 3 minutes. Add the whole garlic clove, together with the beans and cook for 1–2 minutes. Stir in the potatoes and pour in the stock. Cover and cook over a low heat for about 30 minutes. Add the peas and cook for a further 10 minutes.

3. Meanwhile, hard-boil the eggs for about 8–10 minutes. Put them into cold water, then peel and cut them in half lengthways. Season the vegetables with a little salt and pepper and stir in the cinnamon and ground cloves. Transfer to a warm serving dish, garnish with the eggs and serve immediately.

Above: Spinach with raisins and pine nuts
Below: Beans and peas Mallorca-style

Stuffed peppers

Pimientos rellenos guipuzcoanos

Rather time-consuming

Serves 4

45 ml/3 tablespoons olive oil
150g/5 oz minced pork
150g/5 oz minced beef
200 ml/7 fl oz milk
1 bread roll
1 onion
1 clove garlic
4 small peppers
200 ml/7 fl oz sherry
salt and freshly ground black pepper

- Approximately preparation time: 1 hour 20 minutes

Approximately per portion:
1,100 kJ/260 kcal
21 g protein, 11 g fat
17 g carbohydrate

1. Heat 30 ml/2 tablespoons of the olive oil in a frying pan. Add the minced pork and minced beef and fry over a low heat, stirring frequently, for about 5 minutes.

2. Warm the milk in a saucepan. Cut the bread roll into chunks, put them in a bowl and pour the lukewarm milk over them. As soon as the bread is soft, squeeze it out well and rub it through a strainer.

3. Chop the onion, add it to the meat and fry, stirring frequently, until it is soft and translucent. Stir in the bread. Finely chop the garlic and add it to the pan. Season to taste with salt.

4. Cut the 'lids' off the peppers, leaving the stalks on, and core them. Brush an ovenproof dish with some of the remaining oil. Stuff the peppers with the meat mixture and arrange them upright in the dish in a single layer. Pour the remaining oil over them and put their 'lids' back on.

5. Cook in a preheated oven at 200°C/400°F/ Gas 6, basting frequently with the oil, for about 45 minutes, until the skins begin to char and blister.

6. Remove the dish from the oven. Pour on the sherry and return the peppers to the oven for a further 8 minutes. Serve immediately.

Aubergines with honey

Berenjenas con miel

Exquisite

Serves 4

2 eggs
60–75 ml/4–5 tablespoons plain flour, plus extra for dusting
2 medium aubergines
60 ml/4 tablespoons olive oil
115 g/4 oz clear honey
salt and freshly ground black pepper

- Approximate preparation time: 1 hour 35 minutes of which 1 hour is standing time

Approximately per portion:
1,900 kJ/450 kcal
8 g protein, 30 g fat
36 g carbohydrate

1. Lightly beat the eggs and mix them with the flour. Gradually add a little cold water to form a fairly liquid batter. Season the batter with salt and pepper and set aside for about 1 hour.

2. Cut the aubergines into slices about 5 mm/¼ inch thick. Put about 1 litre/1¾ pints lightly salted water in a saucepan and bring to the boil. Add the aubergines and boil for about 3 minutes. Remove them from the heat and drain thoroughly.

3. Pat the aubergines dry with kitchen paper. Spoon a little flour on to a plate. Dip the aubergine slices first in the flour and then in the batter, draining off any excess. Heat the olive oil in a large frying pan and fry the aubergine slices, a few at a time, for about 3 minutes on each side, until they are golden brown. Drain on kitchen paper and keep warm while you fry the remaining slices. Arrange them on a plate and spread a little honey over each slice. Serve at once.

Above: Stuffed peppers
Below: Aubergines with honey

Fried bananas

Plátanos fritos

Quick

Serves 4
6 small Canary bananas or
4 large bananas
50 g/2 oz butter
30 ml/2 tablespoons sugar
2.5 ml/¹/2 teaspoon ground
   cinnamon
¹/4 litre Moscatel or other sweet
   dessert wine
whipped double cream,
   to decorate

- **Approximately per portion:**
  1,300 kJ/310 kcal
  2 g protein, 11 g fat
  40 g carbohydrate

- Approximate preparation
  time: 15 minutes

1. Peel the bananas. Leave small
bananas whole, cut larger ones in
half lengthways. Heat the butter in
a frying pan, but do not allow it to
turn brown.

2. Sprinkle the bananas with sugar.
Add to the pan and fry them in
the butter over a low heat for
about 5 minutes, until they are light
brown. Sprinkle the bananas with
the cinnamon, pour the wine over
them and cook, uncovered, over a
low heat for a further 5 minutes.

3. Arrange the bananas on
individual serving plates and pour
over the warm liquid from the
frying pan. Serve immediately,
decorated with a swirl of stiffly
whipped double cream.

Catalan cream

Crema catalana

Good value

Serves 4
15 ml/1 tablespoon cornflour
500 ml/17 fl oz milk
1 vanilla pod
4 egg yolks
115 g/4 oz sugar
¹/2 cinnamon stick
sugar, for caramelizing

- **Approximately per portion:**
  1,400 kJ/330 kcal
  11 g protein, 17 g fat
  35 g carbohydrate

- Approximate preparation
  time: 35 minutes

1. Stir together the cornflour and
30–45 ml/2–3 tablespoons of the
milk to make a smooth paste.
Bring the remaining milk to the
boil, together with the slit vanilla
pod. Beat together the egg yolks
and sugar until pale and fluffy. Stir
in the milk.

2. Pour the mixture into the
saucepan. Stir in the cornflour
paste and add the cinnamon. Heat,
stirring constantly, until thickened.
Remove the vanilla pod and the
cinnamon stick.

3. Pour the custard into a mould
and, when cold, chill in the
refrigerator. Before serving, heat
some sugar in a little warm water
until it has caramelized. Turn out
the custard on to a serving plate
and pour the caramel over it.
Serve cold.

Apricot cream

Crema de albaricoques

Easy

Serves 4
15 ml/1 tablespoon chopped
   blanched almonds
500 g/1 ¹/4 lb very ripe apricots
50 g/2 oz icing sugar
150 ml/¹/4 pint double cream, plus
   extra to decorate

- **Approximately per portion:**
  990 kJ/240 kcal
  3 g protein, 13 g fat
  27 g carbohydrate

- Approximate preparation
  time: 25 minutes

1. Dry-fry the almonds in a heavy-
based frying pan, stirring constantly,
then remove the pan from the
heat. Stone the apricots, cut into
quarters and peel. Put the apricots
in a food processor and process to
a purée.

2. Mix together the apricot purée
and the icing sugar. Beat the cream
until stiff, then carefully fold it into
the purée.

3. Spoon the apricot cream into
dessert dishes and sprinkle with
the almonds. Decorate with a swirl
of whipped cream and serve at
once. Alternatively, store in the
refrigerator until required and
decorate just before serving.

Above: Fried bananas
Centre: Apricot cream
Below: Catalan cream

Fig tart with almonds

Tarta de higos con almendras

Exquisite

Makes one 25 cm/10 inch tart
500 g/1 1/4 lb puff pastry, frozen
200 g/7 oz ground almonds
150 g/5 oz caster sugar
2 eggs, separated
500 g/1 1/4 lb ripe figs
oil, for greasing

- Approximately preparation
  time: 1 hour 10 minutes

Approximately per portion for 12 slices:

1,300 kJ/310 kcal
7 g protein, 19 g fat
31 g carbohydrate

1. Thaw the puff pastry. Mix together the ground almonds and sugar and fold in the egg whites. Peel the figs and cut them in half.

2. Brush a 25 cm/10 inch loose-based flan tin with oil. Roll out the puff pastry on a lightly floured work surface. Line the prepared tin with it, form a 2.5 cm/1 inch border all around and trim off the excess. Prick the base several times with a fork. Set the remaining pastry aside.

3. Spread half the almond and sugar mixture over the pastry base. Arrange the figs on top, cut side down. Finally, spread the remaining almond mixture on top.

4. Cut the remaining puff pastry

into 1 cm/1/2 inch wide strips and arrange them in a lattice pattern on top of the tart. Beat the egg yolks and brush the pastry lattice to glaze.

5. Bake in a preheated oven at 230°C/450°F/Gas 8 for 25–30 minutes, until golden and cooked through. If necessary, cover the top of the tart with foil after 15 minutes to prevent the pastry from burning. Serve warm.

Apple tart with brandy

Tarta de manzana al coñac

Easy

Makes one 25 cm/10 inch tart
300 g/11 oz puff pastry, frozen
1 kg/2 1/4 lb apples
3 eggs
115 g/4 oz sugar
45 ml/3 tablespoons brandy
150 g/5 oz ground almonds
150 g/5 oz apricot jam
oil, for greasing

- Approximate preparation
  time: 1 hour

Approximately per portion for 12 slices:

1,400 kJ/330 kcal
6 g protein, 18 g fat
35 g carbohydrate

1. Thaw the puff pastry. Peel and core the apples. Cut them into 5 mm/1/4 inch rings.

2. Roll out the puff pastry on a lightly floured work surface. Brush

a 25 cm/10 inch loose-based flan tin with oil and line it with the pastry, forming a 2.5 cm/1 inch border all around. Trim off and discard the excess.

3. Beat together the eggs, 75 ml/5 tablespoons of the sugar and 30 ml/2 tablespoons of the brandy until pale and fluffy. Stir in the ground almonds.

4. Spread the egg mixture over the pastry base. Cut the apple rings in half and arrange the slices in concentric circles on top. Sprinkle the apples with the remaining sugar. Bake the tart in a preheated oven at 220°C/425°F/Gas 7 for about 20 minutes.

4. Heat the jam in a small saucepan until it melts, then rub it through a strainer and mix it with the remaining brandy. Remove the tart from the oven and spread the jam glaze over the apples. Return the tart to the oven and bake for a further 10 minutes, until it has finished cooking. Serve lukewarm or cold.

Above: Fig tart with almonds
Below: Apple tart with brandy

A

almonds: chicken with almond
sauce 46
fig tart with almonds 60
anchovies: marinated anchovies 8
tomato bread with anchovy
fillets 8
apple tart with brandy 60
apricot cream 58
aubergines: aubergine moulds 52
with cheese 52
with honey 56

B

baked fish 36
baked pasta rolls 26
bananas, fried 58
Barcelona fish hotpot 22
Basque-style omelette 24
beans: beans and peas Mallorca-
style 54
lamb stew with haricot
beans 20
beef: spicy meatballs 12
black rice 30
bread: tomato bread with anchovy
fillets 8
bream: baked fish 36
gilt-headed bream in a salt
crust 32
sea bream Madrid-style 32

C

Catalan cream 58
cheese, aubergines with 52
chick pea hotpot 20
chicken: chicken croquettes 12
paella campesina 29
rice paella con caracoles 29
roast chicken with
vegetables 46
with almond sauce 46
with crayfish 48
chorizo: paella campesina 29
clams: shellfish with yellow
sauce 40

G

gilt-headed bream in a salt crust 32

D

drinks 5

E

eggs: Basque-style omelette 24
Spanish-style potato
tortilla 24

F

fig tart with almonds 60
fish: baked fish 36
Barcelona fish hotpot 22
fisherman's stew 22
gilt-headed bream in a salt
crust 32
hake with green sauce 34
marinated anchovies 8
Minorcan fish soup 18
monkfish soup 16
monkfish fisherman-style 36
paella 28
paella del mar 29
sea bream Madrid-style 32
tomato bread with anchovy
fillets 8
trout Pyrenean-style 35
tuna with tomatoes and
peppers 10
fisherman's stew 22
fried squid 38
fried bananas 58
fruit: apple tart with brandy 60
apricot cream 58
fig tart with almonds 60
fried bananas 58

N

nuts: chicken with almond
sauce 46
fig tart with almonds 60
pigs' trotters with pine nuts 50
spinach with raisins and pine
nuts 54

O

omelette, Basque-style 24
onion soup 18

H

cooked vegetable salad 14
crayfish, chicken with 48
cream: apricot cream 58
Catalan cream 58
croquettes, chicken 12
culinary regions 4

H

hake with green sauce 34
ham: paella campesina 29
historical influences 5
honey, aubergines with 56
hotpot, Barcelona fish 22
chick pea 20

L

lamb: leg of lamb Castillian-style 42
paella 28
stew with haricot beans 20
leg of lamb Castillian-style 42
lemon potatoes 10

M

macaroni Basque-style 26
marinated anchovies 8
meat: leg of lamb Castillian-
style 42
pigs' trotters with pine nuts 50
stuffed peppers 56
tripe Madrid-style 50
veal with peppers 43
meatballs, spicy 12
Minorcan fish soup 18
mixed salad 14
monkfish: monkfish fisherman-
style 36
monkfish soup 16
moulds, aubergine 52
mussels: mussels Catalan-style 40
shellfish with yellow sauce 40

P

paella 28
  campesina 29
  con caracoles 29
  del mar 29
pasta: baked pasta rolls 26
macaroni Basque-style 26
peas: beans and peas Mallorca-style 54
peppers: stuffed peppers 56
  tuna with tomatoes and peppers 10
  veal with peppers 43
pigs' trotters with pine nuts 50
pine nuts, pigs' trotters with 50
  spinach with raisins and 54
pork: paella 28
  pigs' trotters with pine nuts 50
  spicy meatballs 12
potatoes: Spanish-style potato tortilla 24
  lemon potatoes 10

R

rabbit: rice paella con caracoles 29
  rice with rabbit 44
raisins: spinach with raisins and pine nuts 54
rice: black rice 30
  paella 28
  paella campesina 29
  paella con caracoles 29
  paella del mar 29
  rice Cuban-style 30
  rice with rabbit 44
roast chicken with vegetables 46

S

salad, cooked vegetable 14
  mixed 14
salt crust, gilt-headed bream in a 32
sauce: chicken with almond sauce 46
  hake with green sauce 34
  shellfish with yellow sauce 40
sea bass: baked fish 36
sea bream Madrid-style 32
seafood: Barcelona fish hotpot 22
  chicken with crayfish 48
  fisherman's stew 22
  fried squid 38
  mussels Catalan-style 40
  paella 28
  paella del mar 29
  shellfish with yellow sauce 40
  small grilled squid 38
shellfish with yellow sauce 40
small grilled squid 38
snails: rice paella con caracoles 29
soup, Minorcan fish 18
  monkfish 16
  onion 18
Spanish eating customs 6
  cena 6
  festivals and special occasions 6
Spanish-style potato tortilla 24
spicy meatballs 12
spinach with raisins and pine nuts 54
squid: fried squid 38
  small grilled squid 38
starters 8–15
stew, fisherman's 22
  lamb stew with haricot beans 20
stuffed peppers 56

T

tapas 8–15
tarts: apple tart with brandy 60
  fig tart with almonds 60
tomato bread with anchovy fillets 8
  tuna with tomatoes and peppers 10
tortilla, Spanish-style potato 24
tripe Madrid-style 50
trout Pyrenean-style 35
tuna with tomatoes and peppers 10

V

veal: spicy meatballs 12
  with peppers 43
vegetables: aubergine moulds 52
  aubergines with cheese 52
  aubergines with honey 56
  beans and peas Mallorca-style 54
  chick pea hotpot 20
  cooked vegetable salad 14
  lamb stew with haricot beans 20
  lemon potatoes 10
  onion soup 18
  roast chicken with vegetables 46
  Spanish-style potato tortilla 24
  spinach with raisins and pine nuts 54
  stuffed peppers 56
  tomato bread with anchovy fillets 8
  tuna with tomatoes and peppers 10

Great Little Cook Books

Spanish Cooking

Published originally under the title
Spanisch kochen by Gräfe und
Unzer Verlag GmbH, München

© 1991 by Gräfe und Unzer Verlag
GmbH, München

English-language edition
© 1998 by Transedition Limited,
Oxford, England

This edition published by

Aura Books plc

Translation:
Translate-A-Book, Oxford

Editing:
Linda Doeser

Typesetting:
Organ Graphic, Abingdon

10 9 8 7 6 5 4 3 2 1
Printed in Dubai

ISBN 1 901683 17 6

Note:
For all recipes, ingredients are given in metric and imperial measurements. Follow only one set, as they are not interchangeable.

Marianne Kaltenbach

has been writing cookery books for over 20 years and has frequently received prizes from the Gastronomic Academy of Germany. She also regularly writes about cooking for various newspapers. She is joint proprietor of a private cookery school and also regularly runs her own cookery courses.

Odette Teubner

was taught by her father, the internationally renowned food photographer, Christian Teubner. At present, she works exclusively in the Teubner Studio for Food Photography. In her spare time she is an enthusiastic painter of children's portraits. She uses her own son as a model.

Kerstin Mosny

studied photography at a college in French-speaking Switzerland. After that she worked as an assistant to various photographers, including the food photographer, Jürgen Tapprich in Zürich. She now works in the Teubner Studio for Food Photography.